A Special Gift

Presented to:

....

From:

....

Date:

....

Stories, sayings, and Scriptures to Encourage and Inspire

hugs™

for the holidays

Stories by
JOHN WILLIAM SMITH
Personalized Scriptures by
LEANN WEISS

HOWARD BOOKS
A DIVISION OF SIMON & SCHUSTER
New York   London   Toronto   Sydney

Our purpose at Howard Books is to:

- *Increase faith* in the hearts of growing Christians
- *Inspire holiness* in the lives of believers
- *Instill hope* in the hearts of struggling people everywhere

Because He's coming again!

Published by Howard Books, a division of Simon & Schuster, Inc.
1230 Avenue of the Americas, New York, NY 10020
www.howardpublishing.com

Hugs for the Holidays © 1997 by John William Smith

The previous printing was catalogued as follows:

Library of Congress Cataloging-in-Publication Data
Hugs for the holidays : stories, sayings, and scriptures to encourage and inspire / stories by John William Smith ; personalized scriptures by LeAnn Weiss.

    p. cm.
    10 Digit ISBN: 1-878990-74-8
    10 Digit ISBN: 1-4165-3402-4
    1. Christmas-Meditations. 2. Christmas stories, American.
I. Weiss, LeAnn. II. Title.
    BV45.S485 1997
    242'.355-dc21

                            97-39667
                              CIP

22 21 20 19 18 17 16 15 14 13

HOWARD is a registered trademark of Simon & Schuster, Inc.

Manufactured in the United States of America

For information regarding special discounts for bulk purchases, please contact: Simon & Schuster Special Sales at 1-800-456-6798 or business@simonandschuster.com.

Stories by John William Smith, author of *My Mother's Favorite Song*, *My Mother Played the Piano*, and contributor to other *Hugs* books.

Scriptures paraphrased by LeAnn Weiss, owner of Encouragemnt Company, 3006 Brandywine Dr., Orlando, Florida 32806.

Edited by Philis Boultinghouse
Cover design by LinDee Loveland
Interior design by LinDee Loveland

contents

v

one

the gift of kindness

*L*ook for me throughout your day! I was hungry and you fed me; I was thirsty and you gave me refreshments; I was a stranger and you showed me hospitality and made me feel welcome. You met my needs when I needed clothes and looked after me with TLC when I was sick. You sacrificed time and visited me when I was in prison or shut-in. Don't miss the opportunities I place before you to meet me! Remember, whatever you do for one of the least of these brothers of mine, you do for me.

Love,

Emmanuel, God with You

Matthew 25:35–40

At this time of year, you are most certainly making a list and checking it twice so you'll know what to look for when you go shopping. You do it every year. It's smart. Otherwise, you might miss someone or something you are supposed to remember. This year, just so you won't forget, write this at the top of the list: "Look for Jesus everywhere."

If you look, you'll see Him. The spirit of Christ is everywhere during the holidays. That's why we love this time of year so much. That's why we hear the endless quotes and comments about how nice it would be if everyone could have the Christmas spirit all year long. It is during these weeks, between Thanksgiving and Christmas, that we experience the heart and spirit of Jesus.

You can see Him in the extra expressions of courtesy and kindness in some of your fellow shoppers. You can see Him on the road as a ride is given to a cold and hungry hitchhiker trying to get home to see his family. You'll recognize Him in hospital volunteers handing out gifts to seriously ill children, some of whom will go to be with Him before His birthday arrives. And there He is again in the smiles of those same children, as they receive their gifts.

Once you start noticing, you'll be amazed at all the shapes and forms he takes. His spirit is there in the bell ringers, soup-kitchen servers, carolers, and helpers of the homeless. He's right there in the bright smile of an expectant child, the tears of a proud mother, and the embrace between longing parents and a prodigal son or daughter who's been called home by a still small voice. And when you look into a mirror, don't be surprised if you see the sparkle of His spirit staring back at you.

Perhaps this is one item you can keep on your list all year long – "Look for Jesus everywhere."

I expect to pass through this world but once; any good thing therefore that I can do, or any kindness that I can show to any fellow creature, let me do it now, let me not defer or neglect it, for I shall not pass this way again.

—John Wesley

Jesus comes in many ways.
That Christmas, he came
to me in the form of a
freezing soldier trying to
get home.

seeing Jesus

In 1962 I was preaching in Indianapolis, Indiana. I was single, and it was Christmas time. I was headed home to Michigan to enjoy the holidays with my family. It was an extremely cold day, and it was snowing. The wind was howling out of the North, blowing thick clouds of fine flakes across the road – it looked like a blizzard. The roads were icy in places, and there was little traffic. Somewhere near Ft. Wayne, Indiana, I saw a soldier standing under an overpass. He had a green army cap pulled as tight and low as possible over his head, his collar was pulled up around his ears, his hands were shoved down in his pockets, and he had a stuffed duffel bag standing beside him.

I was driving a Chevrolet Corvette, and I was going very fast – faster than I should have been, considering the road conditions. As I sped by, the soldier jerked one hand out of his pocket and raised his thumb. My Corvette had two seats – not a front and back seat, but two seats side by side – and I was in one of them. The trunk was big enough to hold three loaves of bread and a pound of lunch meat. Not only was my limited trunk space stuffed full with the clothes and boots I would need for my stay in Michigan, the front seat was stacked high as well, with the presents that I had purchased for my folks and my nieces and nephews.

When I saw the soldier, I was going much too fast to stop, and I was well down the highway before I gave it much thought. I told myself that I couldn't possibly get him and his duffel bag in the car – I debated about the terrible inconvenience and delay it would cause if I did, and by the time I decided that perhaps I ought to at least *offer* to help, I was two miles down the road and out of sight. But my Christian conscience really went to work on me. It was so cold, traffic was almost nonexistent – he was a soldier – and it was Christmas. The inner battle raged for another three miles. Finally,

I decided I would never get any peace unless I offered to help, so I made a U-turn and went back. I hoped with all my heart that someone else had picked him up. That way, I could satisfy my conscience and not be inconvenienced –

wouldn't that be great?

But he was still there, looking more forlorn, lonely, and cold than ever. I was disgusted. I pulled up and rolled down the window. He came running, stumbling on his numb feet, dragging the duffel bag. He leaned over and stuck his head in the window. His face was bluish, his teeth were chattering, his eyebrows and eyelashes were matted with frozen snow, and he could scarcely speak intelligibly.

"Thanks so much for stopping," he said. "I had about given up hope."

That was not what I wanted to hear.

"Where are you going?" I asked, hoping that it was in some direction that would alleviate me from further responsibility.

the gift of kindness

"I live in Michigan, in Taylor Township," he said hopefully. That was really discouraging. It wasn't *directly* on my way, but it wasn't too much out of my way either.

"I'm going to Royal Oak," I said reluctantly.

"Oh," he said, "I know where that is. That's great! If I could just ride with you to Ann Arbor, it would mean a lot to me. I'm almost frozen; I can't feel my ears or feet any more," he said plaintively.

"I don't think I can possibly get both you and your things in," I said.

"If you'll let me, I'll get in – I promise you. I've been standing here for three hours."

I told him to try getting in, and we began rearranging things. The duffel bag was almost as big as he was, and there was only one place for it – the passenger seat. No matter how he put it in the car, he couldn't get in himself. I suggested that maybe he could hide it somewhere and come back for it later. He said he couldn't possibly do that; it had his kids' Christmas presents in it, and he wasn't going anywhere without it. I finally got out, walked around the car, and told him to sit in the passenger seat. As he sat there, I wedged the duffel bag between his legs and between the floor and the roof of the car, I sandwiched all of my presents around him – and I slammed the door. He couldn't move, he couldn't see out either the windshield or his side window – but he was in. I still don't know how we did it.

Once he began to get warm, he began to talk. I found out he was stationed at Fort Leonard Wood, Missouri.

"Didn't I see you go by about five minutes ago?" he asked. I really felt stupid.

"Yes," I said very matter-of-factly.

"You mean you turned around and came back?" I nodded an affirmative.

"Why would you do that?" I paused a long moment.

"Well, you see, I was raised in a home where helping people who were in need was very important. In addition, I'm a minister – actually, it's more than that – I'm a Christian, and if it weren't for that, I'd probably

the gift of kindness

still be going. I have as hard a time doing the right thing as most folks. I fought with this decision for five miles – it's Jesus who makes me do things like turn around and come back. When I don't do the right thing, I have this feeling He's looking at me, and He's so disappointed that I can't stand it."

"Oh!" he said. "You don't know how that convicts me. I'm going to tell you something I never thought I'd tell anybody. I'm no Christian, but my wife is the best person in the whole world, and she goes to church all the time and takes the kids. Truthfully, I've done everything I could to discourage her, but she just keeps going. She's all the time trying to get me to go, telling me that someday I'm going to wish I had.

"Do you know why I'm here hitchhiking? Let me tell you a little story. I was turned down for holiday leave because I got drunk and caused some trouble at the base. I was sick about it. I haven't seen my wife and kids for six months. A friend of mine, who's single, found out at the last minute that his folks were coming to visit some relatives who live close to the base during the holidays. He went to our commanding officer and volunteered to take my duty, if he would let me go home.

"He gave me permission, but I had spent all my money buying presents, which I was going to mail home, so I decided to start hitchhiking. My family doesn't even know I'm coming. I wasn't sure I'd make it, and I didn't want to disappoint them. I've been standing there for three hours, thinking. I watched folks drive by, and it occurred to me that some of them must be Christians, and it made me feel pretty bitter – until I got to thinking about what a lousy person I am, and I knew if I was them, that I probably wouldn't stop either.

"Let me tell you something embarrassing – I got so cold, so lonely, and so desperate that I started to pray – honest to God I did – it was so humiliating. I told God that if he would help me, I'd do better. And you know what? About that time you showed up, and you told me that you came back because of Jesus – now what do you make of that?"

the gift of kindness

"Well, first I'd say that maybe there's more to Christianity than either of us thought, and second, I'd say you'd better start doing better."

I found out exactly where he lived, and we agreed that I could get him pretty close before I had to go in another direction. I think I knew what I was going to do long before I actually said anything. As we approached the intersection where I was going to let him out, I told him that I had made up my mind to take him home.

About two hours later, we pulled up in his driveway. It was almost dark. He was really excited. He asked me to blow my horn, and I did. A few minutes passed, and the inside door opened slowly. The glass in the outside door was frosted over, and whoever was looking out could only tell that there was a car in the driveway. The outside door opened, and a five- or six-year-old, bare-footed, pajamaed boy peeked around the door. When he saw my sports car, he came out on the porch and peered intently at us. His dad opened the door and stepped out.

seeing Jesus

"Hi, David, it's Daddy; I'm home for Christmas!"

He started to say more, but the boy had seen the uniform and heard the voice. The boy's face lit up, and he turned back into the house. I could hear him distinctly – "Mama, Daddy's home," he yelled shrilly. "Daddy's home! Mama! Mama! Daddy's home for Christmas!"

The door opened again, and it didn't open slowly this time – it was thrown open. A woman dressed in a bathrobe and house slippers came running down the steps, her hair flying in the wind, oblivious to the snow and the cold, eyes and mouth opened wide with excitement, with joy etched in every line of her face. "Oh, Carl," she said, "Oh, Carl, you're home. Praise God, you're home. The kids and I have been praying every day that, somehow, God would send you home."

She was followed by a skinny, fair-haired, ten-year-old girl and finally by a tow-headed, blanket-toting, two- or three-year-old girl. They kissed and hugged and laughed and cried, and they danced in the cold and the snow until the soldier finally disentangled himself from them long enough to introduce me.

the gift of kindness

"This is John," he said. "He's a minister, and he's also a Christian; and if it wasn't for him, I wouldn't be here. And I'm going to tell you something, Sandy, right here and now. I told John that I had promised God that I was going to do better, and I am. I'm going to stop drinking, be a better husband, a better father – a better man – and we're going to start going to church together."

I have never witnessed such gratitude in my life. They all had to hug me and kiss me – even the two-year-old – and they told me what a blessing I was to them and that they owed me a debt they could never pay. I was so embarrassed, because I was so unworthy. I had grudged the whole thing until after we had started talking. I wanted to tell them that I didn't deserve any thanks. I tried to leave, but they simply wouldn't allow it. I had to go in the house. I had to eat something and drink something; I had to accept a gift from them – yes, I *had* to. They would not allow me not to, and the more they did, the better and the worse I felt.

seeing Jesus

I was so embarrassed. You know why? I had just witnessed something private – a family thing – something I wasn't part of, something not meant for outsiders – and, yes, I was – I was embarrassed. And you know what else? I envied Carl. I thought that it must be wonderful beyond description to be loved by a woman like that and missed like that and to be so unworthy – and I think Carl was just beginning to understand what he had. I have learned since then that only those who have come to know and feel the love of God can love the unworthy – and I have also learned that we are all unworthy.

Carl was home. I think that at that moment, home meant more to him, perhaps, than it would ever mean again. And when I got to my home and saw my folks and told them why I was late, they were so proud of me – and I was a little proud of myself. Home was somehow brighter, warmer, more dear to me than it had ever been before.

Every human longing – bound up in the inherent yearning to be loved and to be "home" and to experience the peace and security that "home" signifies – has found its fulfillment in Jesus who said, "I go to prepare a place for you." Everything we ever dreamed of home being – what it was or was not – is in that place. Jesus has given purpose, even to the dream of death, because for those who know God – that is the way home.

> "How silently, how silently,
> the wondrous gift is given.
> So God imparts to human hearts,
> the blessings of His heaven.
> No ear may hear His coming,
> but in this world of sin,
> Where meek souls will receive Him still,
> the dear Christ enters in."

Jesus comes to us in many ways. He came to me in the form of a freezing soldier trying to get home for Christmas. He came to a freezing soldier in the form of a young minister trying to find his way to God. Either one of us could have missed him.

Jesus will come to you this Christmas, too, and His coming will be in an unexpected way –

don't miss him.

holiday memories . . .

two

the gift of faith

*T*he heavens declare my glory and the skies proclaim the works of my hand. In the midst of the hurry, don't leave me out of the equation of your life! Remember . . . in me you live and move and have your very being.

Love,

God

Psalm 19:1 & Acts 17:28

At some point in most every person's life, the question arises. It usually begins as something of an observation, but then it grows to an acute awareness. Finally, it swells uncontrollably to the point that the words are formed by the mouth and spoken – almost angrily.

Where did the magic of the holidays go? When was child-like wonder replaced by anxiety and apathy? How did the spirit of the most wonderful holiday of the year escape my once expectant heart?

The answers are simple.

With the passing of years, the magic of the holidays is crowded out by the all too real world of worries. Childlike wonder is pushed beneath a blanket of self-induced stress. The expectant heart is smothered by a vast array of responsibilities – squeezed into too little time. The result is that our faith in the God of wonder is doused with the cold water of simple human haste.

Can the magic of the holidays be restored
in the heart? Most certainly, and quite simply. Take
some time to enjoy the crisp, winter air and the sparkle
of the holiday season. Reserve a quiet evening to sit by
the fire with loved ones so you can feast on each other's
touch and treasured thoughts. Write down everything
you're thankful for over a three-day period and then read
the list in prayer to God. Renew your amazement at the
most wonderful event in history by reading the biblical
accounts of the birth of Christ. Above all, require yourself to slow down, look up, and ask God to reignite
the light of this beautiful holiday season in your
heart.

You can be assured that he'll do it. No
one loves to surprise his children more
than the creator of Christmas.

The magical dust of
Christmas glittered on the
cheeks of humanity ever
so briefly, reminding us
of what is worth having
and what we were
intended to be.

—Max Lucado

Some might say that the
spirit, ever watchful,
seized this precious
moment to kindle into
flame a thought that had
lain dormant for years.

where did it go?

where did it go?

She really didn't want to go, but she had taken the boy to the holiday pageant because she wanted to be a good mother. It was about what she'd expected – old costumes, missed lines, a hackneyed, trite repeat of familiar words and tunes, and characters played by less than amateurs.

The boy had been fascinated by *the star*. It was the only really well-done piece in the set. Someone had obviously put some time, experience, and thought into it. It revolved, high above the stage, sparkling and twinkling, constantly bringing back even an unwilling gaze. The boy had asked what it was, and she had given the old stock answer.

She was relieved when it was finally over.

It was dark when they left, very dark, and very cold, but it was marvelously clear. She hurried toward the car and regretted that she had had to park so far away. She kept his hand in hers, and when he stumbled, she almost fell with him.

"Watch where you're going," she said – perhaps more crossly than she intended. She stopped to help him to his feet.

"I was looking for the star," he said apologetically.

"Why, there's millions of them," she misunderstood.

"I was looking for *His* star," he corrected.

"Oh, don't be silly, honey. That was just a play – people acting. The star went away long ago. You can't see it anymore."

"Where did it go? How do you know you can't see it anymore?" He was disappointed but continued to look.

"I don't know where it went, honey; it just went away, and that's why you can't see it. Come on now; we've got to hurry."

"Maybe it's that one!" He pointed to a particularly bright, friendly star. "Is that Jesus' star?"

where did it go?

"No, honey, it's not Jesus' star. It's just a bright star."

"But it *could* be His star," he insisted. "Maybe it's come back."

Across her consciousness there flashed *a thought*. Where it came from, who could guess? Some might say that the Spirit, ever watchful, never sleeping, seized this precious moment when her guard was down and kindled into flame a thought, a thought that had lain dormant for years.

"Oh God," she thought, "I wish it *were* His star; I wish it *had* come back –

I wish I could believe in it like I used to."

She did not say it out loud, but it was there – and then it was blotted out by cold, fatigue, and pressing cares – but not completely. It was a prayer, and it was heard in the heart of Him who hears the beating of our hearts and knows our every thought – and who waits for moments like these to work His will in our lives. Before she had thought of what to say to her son, His messengers were speeding faster than light to respond.

the gift of faith

At the boy's insistence, she finally looked up, and there *was* a star! I mean, it was as different from other stars as a bonfire is from a kitchen match. She glanced quickly down at her small son, and the soft, iridescent glow of the star seemed to cast a gentle halo of light all around him. And then it was gone, and she shook her head like one who wishes to make certain of her alertness.

When they got home, she was still troubled by it. She helped the boy undress, and she tucked him in with more care and tenderness than usual. When he asked her to help him with his prayers, she did – and she added a special, new prayer of her own. "Dear Father," she said, "I'm not sure just what happened tonight, but thank you."

When she returned to the living room, her husband, without looking up from the TV, said, "Well, how did it go?"

"If you really cared how it went, you might try going sometime. It went about the same as last year when you didn't go with us – except . . . " and her voice trailed off into silence, and she couldn't find a way of finishing.

He looked up from the show he was watching. "Except what? Did something happen?"

"No, nothing you would be interested in."

"Hey, I'm sorry I didn't go.

Did I miss something?"

"Yes, as a matter of fact, you *did* miss something. You missed being with your son and making him think he is more important than that stupid show. You missed being with me and letting me know that I am more important than that stupid show. You miss a lot of things, Andy, but tonight you missed something – something *really* special."

She paused, her heart beating wildly because she knew she was making a leap into the darkness – but she knew she had to take the chance. She picked up the remote control and flipped the TV off.

"You're really worked up about this, aren't you? Did something happen?"

the gift of faith

"Yes," she said. "Yes, something *did* happen, Andy – at least I think it did, although I'm not sure just what – but it's not what happened that really matters. What matters is that it made me start thinking, and we need to talk."

And they did, you know.
They talked and talked.
And things were never the same again.

At some point in every holiday season, I find myself gazing at the stars. They seem especially close and significant when it's cold and silent. I think I want to see *that* star, at least to imagine the *wonder* of it, as it makes its majestic and purposeful way to its appointed destination. There, where it concentrates its glorious radiance on the holy ground, is where Jesus was born. God, calling to us –

"Look over here.
See my Incarnation."

It's not too hard for me to believe in *that* star. My child's heart, awakened from months of slumber by this blessed season, is fully confident that its guiding light brought those wise men to worship Jesus. I wonder, though – where did it go? Does God still move stars to serve His purpose? Is there yet a light calling us to Bethlehem? Does His star not shine for us because we have grown so mature and practical that we dismiss it, as Scrooge dismissed his ghosts by uttering a *"Humbug!"* of disbelief?

The star was for all to see, but only the wise men were guided by it. When they arrived, they did not find multitudes of seekers who had also followed its light. Perhaps the guiding light of God's special star is there yet, but our eyes are not pointed upward to Him – because we do not believe in stars. Our eyes look inward to our own wisdom and outward to our own light and around us to the light and wisdom of people like ourselves. And all the while, God calls us by His light, pleading with us to look upward to His holiness.

Where did it go?
It's where it's always been.

the gift of faith

This holiday season, while your "child's heart" is awakened, look outward and upward –

and you'll be sure to find it.

holiday memories . . .

the gift of forgiveness

*T*his holiday season, leave your relationship baggage behind for good. Get rid of all bitterness, anger, or any form of resentment or hatred you've carried over the years. Instead, be kind and compassionate to one another, forgiving each other, just as in Christ I freely forgave you!

Love,

Your God of Forgiveness

Ephesians 4:31–32

One of the greatest gifts you can give a loved one, acquaintance, family member, or friend is not something you'll have to buy at an expensive boutique, department store, or gift shop. However, it *will* cost you something of value.

There is no need to place this gift in a beautiful box, wrap it in fine paper, or even place a bow around it. No outward adornment could do it justice. Although this gift has no fragrance, visual brilliance, luxurious allure, or commemorative value, it will be cherished above all other gifts received. It is a gift you have to receive yourself before you can adequately give it to others, and it is given best by those who have received it frequently.

It can be given by way of a hug, kiss, letter, or phone call. But it is best delivered in person and directly. The gift is *forgiveness.*

This treasure refreshes lost love, revives old passions, and renews faltered friendships – and it benefits both the giver and the receiver. But the price of forgiveness is exorbitant. "Self" is the asking price, and few are willing to pay it. But when "self" seems too high a price, when pride protection seems a less painful alternative, when the words "you are forgiven" seem better spent at a later time when they'll cost less, remember that the greatest gift ever given was by someone who paid the ultimate price. Jesus exchanged celestial palaces and a heavenly home for a stable, a stigma, and a cross. With his vast equity, he bought our forgiveness.

Was there ever a finer gift purchased? Was there ever a present more treasured by those who receive it? Once forgiveness is granted or received, you'll know – without a doubt – that it is one of the most wonderful gifts of all.

Friendship flourishes
at the fountain of
forgiveness.

—William A. Ward

The bitterness and sadness that had gathered up in me for all those years gradually washed away. It was marvelously simple.

the great gifts

Christmas is a time for giving – and receiving. It is also a time for *forgiving* – because that's what God did at Christmas – He forgave us. When we didn't even know we needed it – He forgave us through Jesus. Christmas is also a time that calls for *insight* and *understanding,* because without those things, the real meaning will be lost in the noise and hustle. This is a story about Christmas – about giving and receiving – about insight and understanding – and about

forgiveness.

Without Christmas, without the spirit of humility and goodwill generated by our awareness of His coming, this story could not have happened. You must be both a child and an adult to understand this story.

In 1949 I was in the seventh grade at Mary Lyon Junior High in Royal Oak, Michigan. My parents were having a difficult time financially, which was nothing new, but I found myself needing money occasionally, which was something new for me – I mean, I had never needed money before. I wouldn't have known what to spend it on, but now I knew because – I had discovered girls.

I decided to get a paper route. I got a route delivering the Detroit Free Press. I picked up my papers at 5:30 A.M. and delivered them until about 7:15. I hated getting up – in the winter months especially – because it was totally dark the whole time, bitterly cold, and I couldn't ride my bike because of the snow and ice. But I earned the princely sum of eight dollars per week – when I could collect from my customers, that is –

which was almost never.

Of course my customers weren't up when I delivered my papers – which always made me wonder – why does a person want a paper at 5:30 in the morning when they don't get up until 7:30? Anyway, in order to collect, I had to try to catch them in the evening. One of the places I delivered to was an apartment building of several stories. Mostly single people lived there, and they were rarely at home.

The Christmas of 1949 was a *particularly* bad time financially and relationally at home – I didn't know how very bad it was till much later. My mom and dad weren't getting along at all, and we had taken in boarders to supplement our income. Some of them were alcoholics. Occasionally, we'd find one asleep in the bathtub, and not only did they keep us up at night with their shouting, they didn't pay their rent. This made matters worse between my folks because my dad would feel sorry for them and wouldn't insist that they either pay or move out, which made my mother furious – she said she wished he would feel sorry for *her* sometimes.

At Christmas time, we didn't have a tree. My dad had as much pride as anybody, I suppose, so he wouldn't just say that we couldn't afford one. When I mentioned it, my mother said that we weren't going to have one this year, that we couldn't afford one, and even if we could –

it was stupid to clutter up your house with a dead tree. She was very cross and spoke sharply, which was unusual for her, so I didn't bring it up any more. I wanted a tree badly, though, and I thought – in my naive way – that if we had one, everybody would feel better.

About three days before Christmas, I was out collecting for my paper route. It was fairly late – long after dark – it was snowing and very cold. I went to the apartment building to try to catch a customer who hadn't paid me for nearly two months – she owed me seven dollars. Much to my surprise, she was home. She invited me in, and not only did she pay me, she gave me a dollar tip! It was a windfall for me – I now had *eight whole dollars.*

What happened next was totally unplanned. On the way home, I walked past a Christmas tree lot, and the idea hit me. The selection wasn't very good because it was so close to the holiday, but there was this one real nice tree. It had been a very expensive tree, and no one had bought it; now it was so close to Christmas that the man was afraid no one would. He wanted ten dollars for it, but when I – in my gullible innocence – told him I only had eight, he said he might sell it for that. I really didn't want to spend the whole eight dollars on the tree, but it was so pretty that I finally agreed.

I dragged it all the way home – about a mile, I think – and I tried hard not to damage it or break off any limbs. The snow helped to cushion it, and it was still in pretty good shape when I got home. You can't imagine how proud and excited I was. I propped it up against the railing on our front porch and went in. My heart was bursting as I announced that I had a surprise. I got Mom and Dad to come to the front door, and then I switched on the porch light. There was our Christmas tree, with the snow glistening on its branches – our beautiful Christmas tree.

I had saved the day.

"Where did you get that tree?" my mother exclaimed. But it wasn't the kind of exclamation that indicates pleasure.

the gift of forgiveness

"I bought it up on Main Street. Isn't it just the most perfect tree you ever saw?" I said, trying to maintain my enthusiasm.

"Where did you get the money?" Her tone was accusing, and it began to dawn on me that this wasn't going to turn out as I had planned.

"From my paper route." I explained about the customer who had paid me.

"And you spent the *whole eight dollars* on this tree?" she exclaimed.

She went into a tirade about how stupid it was to spend my money on a dumb tree that would be thrown out and burned in a few days. She told me how irresponsible I was and how I was just like my dad with all those foolish, romantic, noble notions about fairy tales and happy endings and that it was about time I grew up and learned some sense about the realities of life and how to take care of money and spend it on things that were needed and not on silly things. She said that I was going to end up in the poorhouse because I believed in stupid things like Christmas trees, things that didn't amount to anything.

I just stood there. My mother had never talked to me like that before, and I couldn't believe what I was hearing. I felt awful, and I began to cry. I didn't *want* to cry, but she was so angry, and her words were just pouring out in a stream that she couldn't seem to stop. Finally, she reached out and snapped off the porch light. "Leave it there," she said. "Leave that tree there till it rots, so every time we see it, we'll all be reminded of how stupid the men in this family are." Then she stormed up the stairs to her bedroom, and we didn't see her until the next day.

My dad tried hard to patch things up. He said that Mom wasn't feeling too good and made all kinds of excuses for her. He said that I shouldn't take what she said too seriously. He said it was just a bad time and that she would be better tomorrow –

but he was wrong –
she wasn't better.

the gift of forgiveness

He and I brought the tree in, and we made a stand for it. He got out the box of ornaments, and we decorated it as best we could; but men aren't too good at things like that, and besides, it wasn't the same without Mom. There were a few presents under it by Christmas day – although I can't remember a single one of them – but Mom wouldn't have anything to do with it. It was the worst Christmas I ever had. The happiest day of that season was the day after Christmas when Dad said he thought it would be best if we took the tree down. We never took our tree down until after New Year's Day, but I didn't argue; I was glad to take it down and get it out of my sight. We burned it in the backyard. Mom never said any more about it – good or bad – but it was a scar on my soul,

and I never forgot.

Judi and I married in August of 1963, and Dad died on October 10 of that year. Over the next eight years, we lived in many places. Mom sort of divided up the year – either living with my sister Jary or with us. In

the great gifts

1971 we were living in Wichita, Kansas – Lincoln was about seven, Brendan was three, and Kristen was a baby. Mom was staying with us during the holidays. On Christmas Eve I stayed up very late. Mom, Judi, and the kids had long since gone to bed with visions of sugarplums dancing in their heads. I was sitting in the living room staring into the blinking lights on our tree and reading Matthew's account of the birth of Jesus. I looked at all of the presents and relived all the Christmases of my past. I was totally alone with my thoughts, alternating between joy and melancholy, and I got to thinking about my paper route, that tree, what my mother had said to me, and how Dad had tried to make things better.

I heard a noise in the kitchen and discovered that it was Mom. She couldn't sleep either and had gotten up to make herself a cup of hot tea – which was her remedy for just about everything. As she waited for the water to boil, she walked into the living room and discovered me there. She didn't say much for a while – she just sat and gazed at the tree, the blinking lights, and all the presents – many of which were from her to our children. She saw my open Bible and asked me what I was reading. When I told her, she asked if I would read it to her, and I did.

"This is how the birth of Jesus Christ came about."

"Read it to me out of the King James," she said. This was no time to argue the merits of translations, and besides, I like to read the King James sometimes. I went and got my King James and read,

"Now the birth of Jesus Christ was on this wise."

I saw her nod of affirmation at the familiar words. "That's better," she said – and it was, you know.

"And they will call His name Immanuel –
which means – God with us."

When the kettle began to whistle, she went and made her tea. She came back, and we started to visit. I told her how happy I was that she was with us for Christmas and how I wished that Dad could have lived to see his grandchildren and to enjoy this time because he always loved Christmas so. It got very quiet for a moment, and then she said, "Do you remember that time on Twelve Mile Road when you bought that tree with your paper route money?"

"Yes," I said, "I've just been thinking about it."

She hesitated for a long moment, as though she were on the verge of something that was bottled up so deeply inside her soul that it might take surgery to get it out. Finally, great tears started down her face, and she cried,

"Oh, son, please forgive me.

"That time and that Christmas have been a burden on my heart for twenty-five years. I wish your dad were here so I could tell him how sorry I am for what I said. Your dad was a good man, and it hurts me to know that he went to his grave without ever hearing me say that I was sorry for that night. Nothing will ever make what I said right, but you need to know that your dad never did have any money sense (which was all too true). We were fighting all the time – though not in

the gift of forgiveness

front of you – we were two months behind on our house payments, we had no money for groceries, your dad was talking about going back to Arkansas, and that tree was the last straw. I took it all out on you. It doesn't make what I did right, but I hoped that someday, when you were older, you would understand. I've wanted to say something for ever so long, and I'm so glad it's finally out."

Well, we both cried a little and held each other, and I forgave her – it wasn't hard, you know. Then we talked for a long time, and I *did* understand; I saw what I had never seen, and the bitterness and sadness that had gathered up in me for all those years gradually washed away.

It was marvelously simple.

The great gifts of this season – or any season – can't be put under the tree; you can't wear them or eat them or drive them or play with them. We spend so much time on the lesser gifts – toys, sweaters, jewelry, the mint, anise, and dill of Christmas – and so little on the

the great gifts

great gifts – understanding, grace, peace, and *forgiveness*. It's no wonder that the holiday leaves us empty, because when it's over, the only reminders we have are the dirty dishes and the January bills.

The great gifts are like *the one gift* – the gift that began it all back there in Bethlehem of Judea. You can't buy them, and they're not on anybody's shopping list. They come as He came – quietly, freely, unexpectedly – and if you're not careful, you'll miss them entirely, because the *want* list will keep you at the mall where the holiday sales, tinsel, background music, and glitter keep you from seeing the star over Bethlehem or hearing the angel's song.

> "How silently, how silently,
> the wondrous gift is given!
> So God imparts to human hearts
> the blessing of His heav'n.
> No ear may hear His coming,
> but in this world of sin,
> Where meek souls will

the gift of forgiveness

receive Him still,
the dear Christ
enters in."
—"O Little Town of Bethlehem"

holiday memories . . .

four

the gift of

assurance

I am faithful to all my promises and loving toward you. My love endures forever, and my faithfulness continues through all generations.

Love,

Your Trustworthy Heavenly Father

Psalm 145:13 & Psalm 100:5

It happened a few months before the first Christmas. A significant message was delivered to Mary, the mother of Jesus – a message she needed to hear, a message you need to hear – on Christmas Day and every day that follows.

Though the message was spoken by her cousin Elizabeth, it had been given to Elizabeth by the Holy Spirit. In other words, the message was not from Elizabeth – it was from God. And it was meant to be remembered – not just by Mary, but also by you and me, and not just for the first Christmas, but for this one too. The message was only one sentence long, but it served as a bold exclamation point in a beautiful and tender exchange between these two treasured women of faith and courage.

On the lips of Elizabeth, God sent this reassurance, *"Blessed is she who has believed that what the Lord has said to her will be accomplished."*

Because of the confusing circumstances Mary found herself in, she must have been struggling with fear and doubt, but God stepped forward and offered warm words of comfort and assurance. He extended His hand to calm the cold clash of faith and doubt, trust and fear, confidence and uncertainty.

He will do the same for you.

If you need His powerful voice to calm your timid heart, He will not hesitate to use it. If you need a show of His strength to defeat the forces of fear, God will act. He feels the pain of his children's doubt. He knows the limits of our strength. He wants you to know his comfort and assurance even in the most disturbing times.

This holiday season and beyond, when the world challenges your faith or pain pulls at your confidence, remember the resounding reassurances of God given to a tender young woman in frightening circumstances: *"Blessed are you who have believed that what the Lord has said to you will be accomplished."*

Christ is coming again!

The smallest seed
of faith is better than
the largest fruit of
happiness.

—Henry David Thoreau

Those marvelous events of childhood were just for me – for me to remember when I have doubts, for me to tell you about when you have doubts.

home for
Christmas

"Then Jesus told his disciples a parable
to show them that they should always pray
and not give up."
—Luke 18:1 NIV

In 1946 we had Christmas dinner at Aunt Velma's.
I was nine. Aunt Velma was my mother's youngest
sister. She was married to my uncle Brett Snoddy –
pronounced, *Snow'-dee*. They were always pretty
touchy about their last name, so I want to make sure
I don't offend them – though I haven't seen any of
them for thirty years, at least.

Aunt Velma had five children – Brett Jr., Bobby,
Sidney, Nancy, and David. David was my age, and

the gift of assurance

Nancy was my sister's age. Brett Jr. and Bobby were much older than I.

In 1946 the Snoddys were living in a log house – it had an open ceiling with big log support beams – it was a fascinating place. Anyway, Brett Jr. and Bobby had been drafted, because of the war, and I had not seen them in a long time – but now the war was over, and they were going to be home for Christmas.

We got there pretty early, and we opened presents. Brett Jr. was there when we got there, but Bobby wasn't, and I could tell that Aunt Velma was upset about it. I heard her tell my mom that Bobby had called and said he was trying to hitchhike home – he didn't have money for a bus.

The day went by pretty quickly for me – we built a huge and elaborate snowman – complete with a carrot nose, charcoal eyes and ears, and a top hat and scarf. Then we had a snowball fight, after which we went ice skating on the creek that ran near their house. By dinnertime, I was famished. Aunt Velma postponed dinner as long as she could – but Bobby didn't show.

Finally, we sat down to eat without him. Aunt Velma set a place for Bobby, and she put a chair for him at the table. I think it sort of made everybody solemn –

looking at that empty chair.

The Snoddy's weren't religious people, and usually they just dove right into whatever was on the table, but today Aunt Velma asked my dad to pray. It took her a minute or two to get it out, but she asked my dad to pray that God would take care of her Bobby and send him home. Her voice was all shaky and choked up, and when I looked at her, I saw that she was crying – the tears were running down her cheeks and

dripping right onto her plate.

Everybody got real sad. We all bowed our heads, but for some reason, my dad didn't get right into his prayer, and when he did, it was a lot different from the one he usually prayed – the one I could say by heart. When he finished, it was pretty quiet for awhile – but then we started passing things and eating and talking, and everybody sort of got loosened up – like you always do

the gift of assurance

– and we laughed and told stories. Even Aunt Velma joined in. It was a great dinner.

We were eating dessert when it happened – I mean, we had totally forgotten –

but He hadn't.

One of the boys said, "Somebody just pulled into the driveway," and everything stopped, but nobody moved. Then a car door slammed, and there was a knock on the door. It's funny how you react to things. Everybody just sat and looked at each other – everybody but Aunt Velma. She was already up serving dessert.

"It's Bobby," she cried, "God has sent Bobby home; I just know He has."

"Now Velma, don't get your hopes up," Uncle Brett said. "It's probably someone else."

Then everybody started to get up, but nobody could beat Aunt Velma to the door. She was determined that it was Bobby –

and it was.

home for Christmas

I don't know what anybody else thought, because we didn't talk about it, but I never doubted for one minute that God had sent Bobby home –

and I still don't doubt it.

I was nine. Sometimes I think those marvelous events were just for me –

for me to remember
when I have doubts,
for me to tell you about
when you have doubts.

holiday memories . . .

the gift
of hope

I am the resurrection and the life.
Anyone who believes in me will live,
even though he dies, and anyone who
lives and believes in me will never die.

Love,

The God

of Everlasting Life

John 11:25–26

It was an event that lasted but a few hours – a spectacular explosion of light on history's timeline – and then it was gone. And yet, its monumental impact is still felt in human hearts today – 2000 years later. If you could ask those who participated in that sacred event, they would tell you that it was the single most important day of their lives.

The young mother who lay on the crudely gathered bed of hay would have other children in her life, but as she nursed the infant and cleaned his skin and cleared his eyes, she knew there would never be another day like today. The rough, strong hands of the earthly father would feel the silkiness of a newborn infant again, but as he lifted this child, he whispered to himself, "There will never be another day like today." Then the shepherds came – still wild eyed from their encounter with angels in the field. When their gaze fell on the sleeping infant king, they looked at each other longingly and, almost in unison, spoke the words once more, "There will never be another day like today."

But within a few hours, the day ended, and the manger was empty –

cleaned of all signs of the spectacular sequence,
except for the indention in the hay where the mother
and baby had slept the deep sleep of exhaustion.

Why does that singular day soften the hearts of a
cynical society and compel the entire world to say there
will never be another day like that one? Because that one
event on that one day was the initiation, the commence-
ment, the birth of *hope* – hope that man could become
one with God, hope that the blind could see, that the
lame could walk, that the hungry could be fed, and above
all, hope that the dead could live once again.

Don't let the wonder of that hope disappear with
the decorations at the end of the holiday season this
year. Follow hope right out of that manger and
into the rest of His life. Watch hope become a
man, the man a lamb, and the lamb the Lord
who will come for us again. When he
comes, we'll look at one another and
say, "There will never be another
day like today."

Hope is the thing with
feathers
That perches in the soul
And sings the tune
without the words
And never stops, at all.

—Emily Dickenson

While she was with us,
she filled our hearts with
hope and reminded us on
Christmas Day "who made
lame beggars walk and
blind men see."

Priscilla's last Christmas

Christmas of 1992, we made our annual pilgrimage to my sister Jary's house in Albany, Georgia. I didn't know at the time how historically significant this Christmas was to be.

One of the real blessings of having Christmas at Jary's house is seeing Priscilla – she's my niece. Priscilla has a neuromuscular disease, which has kept her confined to a wheelchair for thirteen of her twenty-five years.

You need to know two things about Priscilla if you are going to understand what I want to say. First, I have never known her to use her condition as a tool to manipulate people and get what she wants. Second, with all of her physical problems, it would be expected

that she would be totally self-centered – she isn't. Priscilla is thoughtful, patient, sensitive toward others, and full of hope – her relationship with Jesus has made her that way. Whenever Priscilla and I get together, we always take a walk. I push her in her wheelchair, and as we walk, we talk. Talking is very hard for us.

Priscilla has to work very hard to talk, and what she says isn't always as intelligible as she would like, because her condition has affected her speech. To make matters worse, my ears aren't what they used to be, so between the two problems, we really struggle to understand each other. Sometimes I have to ask her two or three times to repeat what she has said. Even people who can speak easily get aggravated with me. Priscilla struggles with every word – but she is patient with me – slowly, painfully, she forces out each syllable to make me understand, and then we laugh about it. That's another thing – she has a great sense of humor and takes teasing unbelievably well –

because she is not vain.

Priscilla's last Christmas

When we took our walk on that Christmas Day, it was obvious to me that her condition had deteriorated. As we strolled through the neighborhood, we were greeted often by friendly people. Priscilla said, "Uncle John, do you think people are more friendly to me because I'm crippled?"

"Yes," I said, "I think they are, and it makes me glad to think so. Most people have more of God in them than they suspect. If you remember, it seems that Jesus always showed special attention to those who had special needs."

Then she asked if I remembered a passage from Charles Dickens' "A Christmas Carol," where Bob Cratchit was telling his wife what Tiny Tim had said to him on the way home from church on Christmas Day.

"He told me, coming home, that he hoped the people
saw him in the church, because he was crippled,
and it might be pleasant to them to remember,
upon Christmas Day,
who made lame beggars walk and blind men see."

the gift of hope

Priscilla told me that she hoped that people would feel the same way about her so that her malady might help folks to be more grateful to God for their health.

As we neared the end of our walk that Christmas Day – as we came in sight of the house – with all the cars parked around it and all our family inside – she said, "I'm so thankful for my family. I just don't know what people do who don't have a family to care for them." That was our last walk and

our last words on this earth.

On Saturday, February 2, 1992, Jary called me and said that Priscilla was in the hospital and that her condition was serious. We got in the car and drove three hundred fifty miles in record time. As I drove, I found myself praying – O God, please let her be alive when I get there. I really don't know why that was so important to me – but it was. We arrived at the hospital about 2:30 A.M. and went directly to ICU.

She was alive.

Priscilla's last Christmas

For the next hour, we cried and prayed as we watched her life slip gradually away. It was as it's supposed to be – your family standing around your bed in your last moments. The little blips on the monitor raced and slowed – raced and slowed, then stopped. There were no more blips, and that meant she was gone. I wouldn't call her back for anything – I am very selfish, but not that selfish –

but I miss her.

Now, at every family Christmas gathering, we are reminded of how blessed we were to have her – and how blessed we are to have each other. We don't take each other for granted anymore, and we don't take Christmas for granted any more. We are made sad by her death, but we are also made glad – because we know that now she walks and talks freely and without pain and because, while she was with us, she filled our hearts with hope and reminded us on Christmas Day

"who made lame beggars walk and blind men see."

holiday memories . . .

the gift of timeless treasures

*B*ecause of my endless love for
you, I didn't spare even my own Son.
I gave Jesus up for you! You can trust
me to graciously give you all things.

Love,
Your God of Every Good
and Perfect Gift

Romans 8:32 & James 1:17

Open your mailbox, pick up the paper, turn on the radio, or power on the television during the holiday season, and you'll be sure to read or hear something about *gifts* – gifts for wives, husbands, kids, bosses, teachers, friends, and far-off relatives. All of these commercials echo the same message. The words may be different, but the promise is the same – they all promise gifts that last, that keep on giving – gifts that will stay in the memory forever. The gift they're selling shines, shares, shows, and glows long after the holiday season is over. It's guaranteed to last a lifetime; it's trusted, treasured, timeless, and tested.

Why do those who sell gifts go to such lengths to convince us that their bobbles, beads, and bangles will endure through time? It's because they know that enduring gifts communicate love and commitment.

I don't know if you have thought about it or not, but you already possess one of the most timeless treasures ever given anyone. Not only is it priceless, it was formed and cast through unimaginable sacrifice, suffering, and self-denial. It was kept safe generation after generation by heavenly force, and even now, it is protected and preserved for the next generation and the one after that. It comes in many different forms, but no matter how it is designed and delivered, this gift is a truly timeless treasure. The gift is God's Word – the Bible.

This timeless gift houses countless other gifts that you can pass on to those who need to partake of its rich content. God's Word overflows with spiritual gifts of life, peace, love, and happiness. Not only do its pages hold ceaseless *spiritual* riches, they also hold unspeakable *power* – power to sustain the weary, heal the sick, mend the brokenhearted, restore lost love, and forgive the fallen. Other gifts make empty promises of vast blessings, but only God's Word lives up to its promise of full and everlasting life. It may be stuck on a table or sitting on a shelf, but it belongs in the human heart, because that's where the maker of the gift intended it to live.

This holiday season, allow God to give this gift to you and to others in your family. Read about the birth of Christ – not just once, but several times. After the holidays are over, open up this world of gifts, which communicates God's love and commitment for you, and read it day after day. This gift is the standard for all other gifts. It is the only one that keeps its promise to last forever.

May life's greatest gifts
always be yours—
happiness, memories,
and dreams.

—unknown

Holding the gift that my
mom's hands had touched
filled me with a sense of
her presence, and hugging
Mildred was like hugging
Mom.

timeless treasures

A few days before Christmas, an elderly lady named Mildred Rhodes asked me to come to her house. Mildred and I have been friends for a long time. I met her in 1969, when I moved to Wichita, Kansas, to work for Maude Carpenter's Children's Home. Mildred's husband, Bill, had been instrumental not only in bringing the children's home into existence, he had given his *life* to it, building it into a widely respected institution. He had died quite suddenly, and the grateful board who ran the home gave Mildred a small apartment there for as long as she wanted it. I came to know her gradually.

About a year after I first met her, I began preaching at a church in Wichita, where Mildred attended with her daughter and son-in-law. My wife and I developed a warm and lasting friendship with her children and grandchildren, and when my mother came to stay with us, it seemed natural for her to develop a relationship with Mildred. Their friendship grew and lasted until my mom died in 1975.

Twenty years passed, we moved several times, and although I seldom saw Mildred, she and my mother remained close. Then we moved to Montgomery, Alabama. Mildred had another daughter and son-in-law who lived there, and she came to live with them. Once again, Mildred and I lived in the same town, and once again, she worshiped where I preached. Every Sunday morning, I looked out into the audience and there was Mildred. I could almost see my mother sitting beside her, and I was reminded of the amazing providence of God.

When I went to Mildred's house, she told me that the reason she had asked me to come by was that she had something she wanted to give me. She walked over to her small Christmas tree and removed an ornament. She placed it in my hands and told me that my mother had given it to her years ago – and now she wanted me to have it. Holding the gift that my mom's hands had touched me with a sense of her presence, and hugging Mildred was like hugging Mom.

In my mind's eye, I imagine that a few days before Christmas, God and Jesus and the Holy Spirit got together and said, "Now, what can we give John for Christmas this year?" And one of them said, "You remember that tree ornament his mother gave to Mildred Rhodes? Why don't we put it in Mildred's heart to give it to him?" And all of them thought that would be the nicest gift ever, and so they worked it out.

Isn't it heartwarming to be reminded of how God does the nicest, most thoughtful things for us - things we could never think of. You know, I suspect that the real pleasure He gets from giving gifts is not so much from hearing us say, "Thank you" – on those few occasions when we are awake enough to know that He has blessed us once again – but from watching us open our presents and seeing the expression of joy and wonder steal softly across our faces and into our hearts – that is what really makes him glad.

the gift of timeless treasures

Mildred is gone now. She died in 1993. We had moved far apart, and I didn't even know that she had died till long after the funeral. I am very sorry to have missed it. I hold her memory in my heart, and it brings joy to me. When I place that ornament on our tree this year, I will be reminded of God's love, and I will experience the joy of his providence once again. I also know that it will give Him great pleasure to watch me once again open my gifts.

holiday memories . . .

the gift
of Jesus

*T*he difference is me! I am
your way, your truth, and your
life. Don't settle for survival; I
came to give you *life!*

Jesus

John 10:10 & John 14:6

You would be blind not to notice it. It happens every year at exactly the same time. About the third week in November, a transition takes place in the world. It is almost as if someone hit a switch – it happens that suddenly. Everyone in the world becomes a little different. Yes, *different* is the perfect word.

Children act differently toward their parents, and parents see their children through different eyes. Smiles come easier, patience is plentiful, and affection seems natural. Society is different too. The man-made gulf between rich and poor, black and white, boss and employee, teacher and student is filled in by feelings of goodwill and God's love. For about thirty days, the pursuits and passions that keep the world spinning at its dizzying pace are put into perspective.

What causes this miraculous transformation to take place? It certainly isn't the dazzling decorations that fill the streets and shop windows. If that were the key, our world would be gaudy with decorations every day. It isn't the falling snow, because the snow continues to fall long after the joy of the season disappears. It isn't family reunions, office parties, brightly wrapped gifts, or the funny pointed trees that seem to magically appear in practically every home, school, and business in the world.

This vast difference in human hearts has been transmitted through 2000 years, from a far-off city few of us have ever seen, from a lonely little manger in which a young virgin miraculously gave birth to a single infant. That infant is the difference.

His name is Jesus.

The coming of Christ by way of a Bethlehem manger seems strange and stunning. But when we take Him out of the manger and invite Him into our hearts, then the meaning unfolds and the strangeness vanishes.

—C. Neil Strait

They came to love Tiny Tim
and Bob Cratchit for the same
reason they loved the story of
Jesus' birth – he was poor
and they were poor; he was
oppressed and so were they.

the difference

When I think of Christmas, I often think of something that happened during my school-teaching days. The school I taught in was very old. It had fourteen-foot ceilings and huge windows. The kids who attended this ghetto school were tough, and they were extremely poor. Maybe that's how they got to be so tough.

Christmas has always been my favorite holiday, and I determined that this year, I was going to try to make it special for my kids.

I got permission from my principal to put a Christmas tree in my classroom. It was a blue spruce. It was twelve feet tall, and it must have been eight or ten feet in circumference. I got two of the boys, Jim and Chris, to help me drag it in and build a stand for it. We put

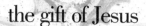

it right in the middle of our classroom. For two or
three days, school was going to take a back seat. I asked
all 120 kids to each bring one ornament from home. I
was surprised at the participation – and the variety.
Some were homemade, but many were new and cheap
– obviously something they had purchased for the
occasion – which meant they probably didn't have any
at home.

Even at this time of year, they were ready to fight at
the drop of a hat. If somebody put their ornament
where somebody else wanted theirs, they would fight.
If somebody knocked one off, there was sure to be a
fight. If somebody didn't bring one – or brought two –
there was a fight. It was a frustrating time for me,
because I wanted Christmas to bring them together –
to teach them kindness –

like it's supposed to.

When the tree was finished, I spent one whole
school day, each period, trying to explain about Christmas – what it meant to me and what I thought it ought

the difference

to be like. I told them that it was against school policy to read the Bible in class, but if they had no objections, I was going to do it anyway. When they found out it was contrary to school policy –

they insisted that it must be read.

On Wednesday I read the gospel accounts of Jesus' birth, and I also began reading *A Christmas Carol,* by Charles Dickens. I could sense that they liked it, although they dared not show it. On Thursday I continued reading Dickens each period until my voice was nearly gone. Many of them were moved. I could tell. In one class, one of the girls began to cry when it appeared that Tiny Tim was going to die – not loudly, but someone noticed and ridiculed her.

"Hey, look, Brenda's crying."

"I am not," she sobbed, "and I'll smash your face if you say I am."

That's when Jim stood up.

Jim was big, very big, and he was tough – but he wasn't mean. He would never sucker-punch a guy, and he didn't go looking for touble. He was painfully slow of mind, he never answered a question, never took a test, never opened his book, and only when I occasionally departed from the lesson to tell a story did I ever notice a flicker of interest.

Jim loved stories.

So when the boy ridiculed Brenda, Jim stood up and grabbed him by the shirt collar. He jerked him out of his seat and held him with his feet about six inches off the floor.

"You shut your filthy, big mouth. Let her cry if she wants to. I might cry myself, and if I do, you'd better start crying, too, or I'll give you something real personal to cry about. Now, I'm gonna hear the rest of this story, and I mean to hear it without no stops." (He meant interruptions.)

The story went on, and there were no interruptions. I believe they came to love Tiny Tim and Bob Cratchit for the same reason they had loved the story of Jesus' birth. He was poor and they were poor, and he was oppressed – the underdog – and they saw themselves as oppressed, as always being the underdogs – and they were. For all their toughness, Jesus and Tiny Tim melted them. They had never had the chance to be children, and when Tiny Tim recovered and Scrooge was humbled, they laughed and clapped their hands and were very pleased.

I believe it made them kinder and gentler with each other. And why shouldn't it? It has done so for me and for a million others. We were not so different – them and me – a few dollars, some social graces, verbal skills, and age.

The real difference
was Jesus.

holiday memories . . .